FULL SCORE

WSL-11-029
＜吹奏楽セレクション楽譜＞

I Was Born To Love You

Freddie Mercury　作曲
郷間幹男　編曲

楽器編成表		
木管楽器	金管・弦楽器	打楽器・その他
Piccolo	B♭ Trumpet 1	Drums
Flutes 1 (& *2)	B♭ Trumpet 2	Percussion 1
*Oboe	*B♭ Trumpet 3	...Shaker,Tambourine
*Bassoon	F Horns 1 (& *2)	*Percussion 2
*E♭ Clarinet	F Horns 3 (& *4)	...Sus.Cymbal,Castanet,
B♭ Clarinet 1	Trombone 1	Wind Chime
B♭ Clarinet 2	Trombone 2	Glockenspiel
*B♭ Clarinet 3	*Trombone 3	*Piano
*Alto Clarinet	Euphonium	
Bass Clarinet	Tuba	
Alto Saxophone 1	Electric Bass	Full Score
*Alto Saxophone 2	(String Bass)	
Tenor Saxophone		
Baritone Saxophone		

＊イタリック表記の楽譜はオプション

I Was Born To Love You

Comp. by Freddie Mercury
Arr. by Mikio Gohma

I WAS BORN TO LOVE YOU
Freddie Mercury
© Copyright by 1984 Mercury Songs Ltd
The rights for Japan licensed to EMI Music Publishing Japan Ltd.

I Was Born To Love You - 3

I Was Born To Love You - 5

I Was Born To Love You - 7

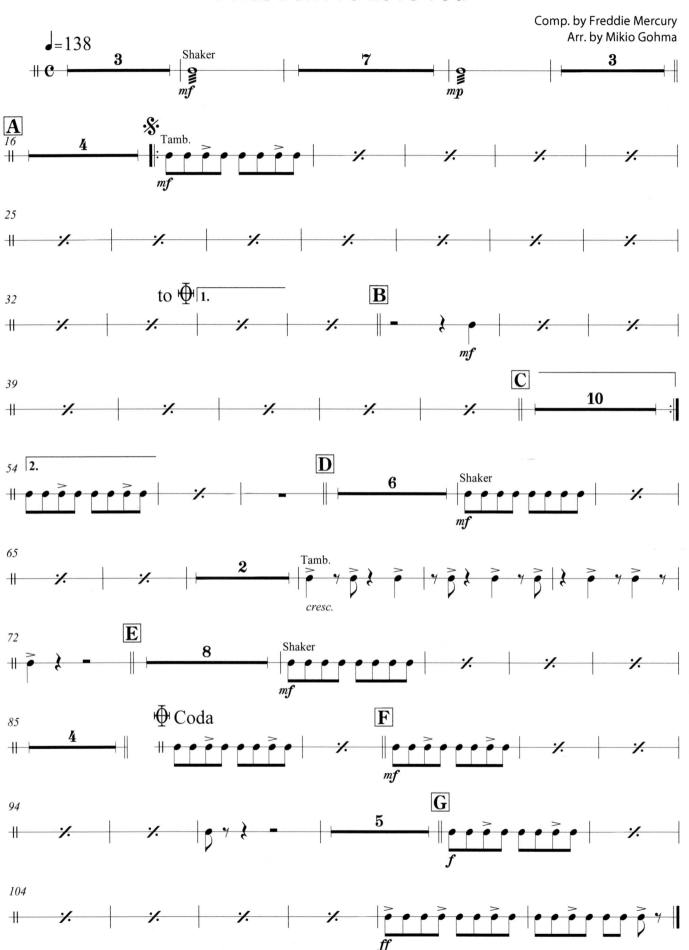

Tuba

I Was Born To Love You

Comp. by Freddie Mercury
Arr. by Mikio Gohma

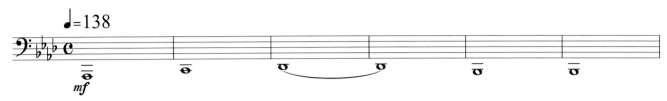

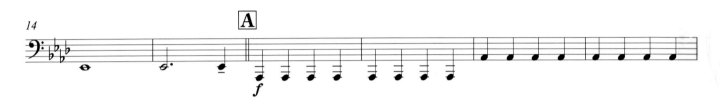

Euphonium

I Was Born To Love You

Comp. by Freddie Mercury
Arr. by Mikio Gohma

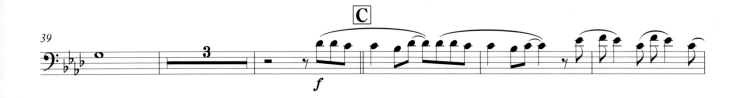

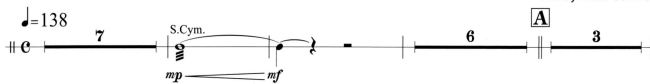
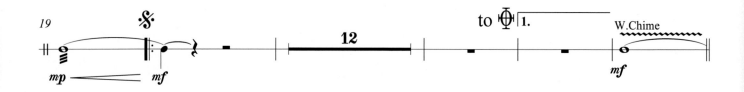

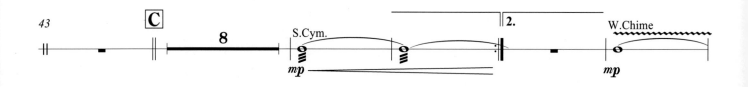
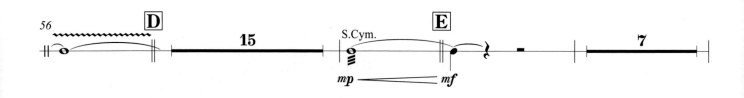
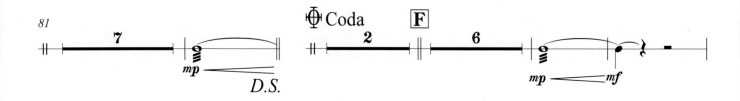

MEMO

Trombone 3

I Was Born To Love You

Comp. by Freddie Mercury
Arr. by Mikio Gohma

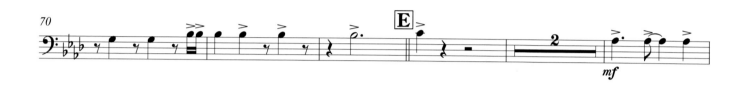

Trombone 2

I Was Born To Love You

Comp. by Freddie Mercury
Arr. by Mikio Gohma

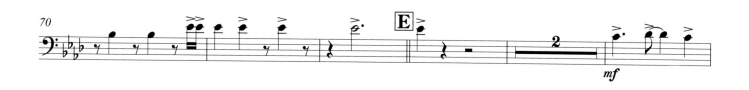

Trombone 1

I Was Born To Love You

Comp. by Freddie Mercury
Arr. by Mikio Gohma

F Horns 3&4

I Was Born To Love You

Comp. by Freddie Mercury
Arr. by Mikio Gohma

F Horns 1&2

I Was Born To Love You

Comp. by Freddie Mercury
Arr. by Mikio Gohma

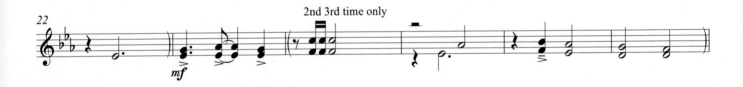

MEMO

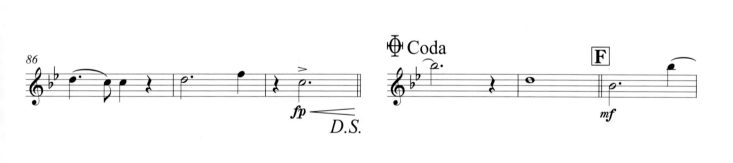

Tenor Saxophone

I Was Born To Love You

Comp. by Freddie Mercury
Arr. by Mikio Gohma

Alto Saxophone 2

I Was Born To Love You

Comp. by Freddie Mercury
Arr. by Mikio Gohma

Alto Saxophone 1

I Was Born To Love You

Comp. by Freddie Mercury
Arr. by Mikio Gohma

MEMO

MEMO

MEMO

I Was Born To Love You

Oboe

Comp. by Freddie Mercury
Arr. by Mikio Gohma

Flutes 1&2

I Was Born To Love You

Comp. by Freddie Mercury
Arr. by Mikio Gohma

MEMO

I Was Born To Love You - 13

ご注文について

ウィンズスコアの商品は全国の楽器店、ならびに書店にてお求めになれますが、店頭でのご購入が困難な場合、当社PC&モバイルサイト・FAX・電話からのご注文で、直接ご購入が可能です。

◎当社PCサイトでのご注文方法

http://www.winds-score.com

上記のURLへアクセスし、WEBショップにてご注文ください。

◎FAXでのご注文方法

FAX.03-6809-0594

24時間、ご注文を承ります。当社サイトよりFAXご注文用紙をダウンロードし、印刷、ご記入の上ご送信ください。

◎電話でのご注文方法

TEL.0120-713-771

営業時間内にお電話いただければ、電話にてご注文を承ります。

◎モバイルサイトでのご注文方法

右のQRコードを読み取ってアクセスいただくか、URLを直接ご入力ください。

※この出版物の全部または一部を権利者に無断で複製(コピー)することは、著作権の侵害にあたり、著作権法により罰せられます。

※造本には十分注意しておりますが、万一落丁乱丁などの不良品がありましたらお取替え致します。また、ご意見ご感想もホームページより受け付けておりますので、お気軽にお問い合わせください。

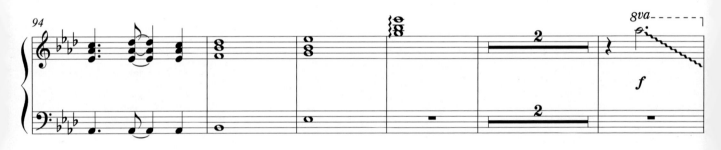